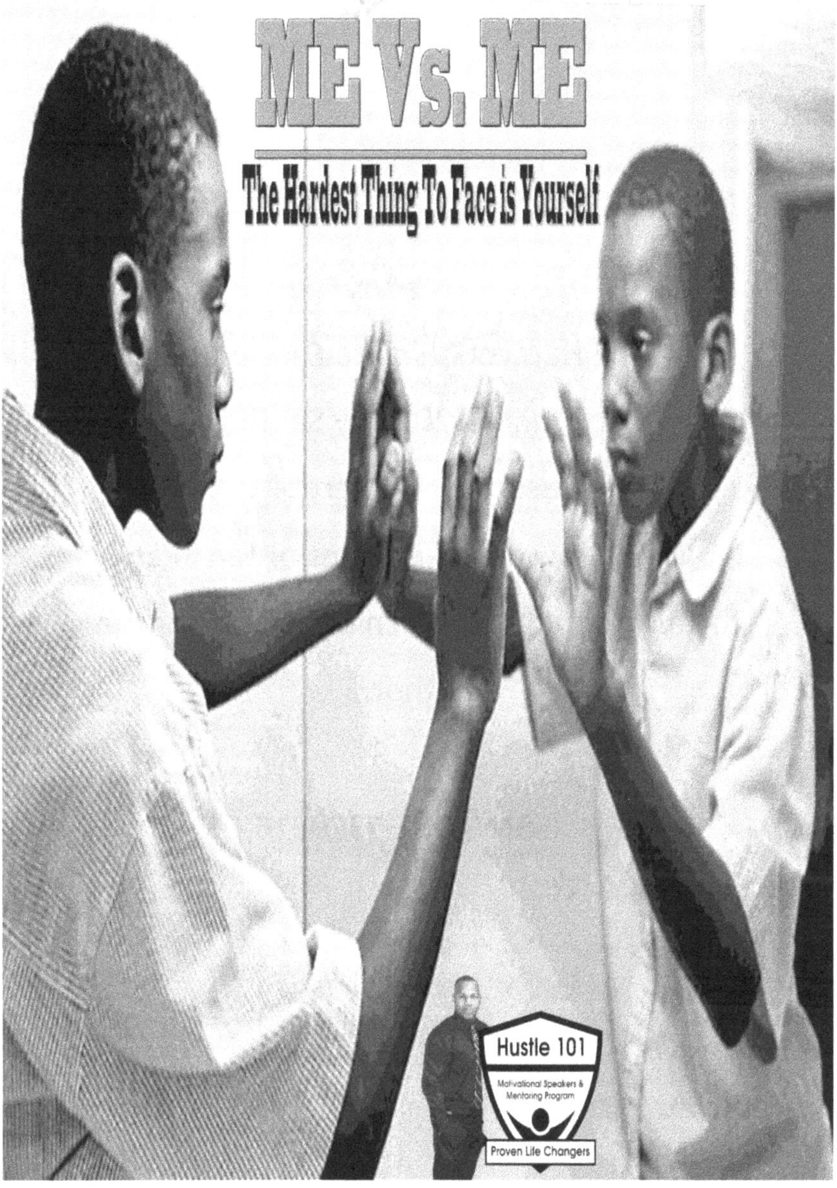
ME Vs. ME
The Hardest Thing To Face is Yourself
Hustle 101
Motivational Speakers & Mentoring Program
Proven Life Changers

Me Vs. Me

(The Hardest Thing to Face Is Yourself)

Copyright © 2021 by Santiego Rivers

All rights reserved. No part of this book may be reproduced or transmitted in any form without the written permission of the author.

ISBN 978-1-7370516-0-2

If there is no enemy within, the enemy outside can do you no harm

When I look in the mirror, I see beyond my reflection and into my soul. I feel the hurt and the pain that hides behind my smile that is getting out of control.

When I look in the mirror, I behold the loneliness and heartache that have burdened my soul. Pain is the journey to happiness, and this is the parable that my elders have told me.

When I look in the mirror, I know that I am fighting for my life every day. I keep moving forward despite the obstacles that stand in my way.

Will I win, or will I lose? I'm fighting a fight that the outcome is uncertain in every way. The one thing that I do know is that I am fighting this battle in my own way.

Come what may, I will face all my monsters and demons until I am the last person standing. Searching outwards has made me look within. There is no mountain higher or no foe greater than the reflection therein.

When I look in the mirror, I know that my battle has begun. I plant my feet and bite down on my teeth because the reasons for quitting there are none.

Table of Content

When I look in the mirror (Spoken Words)

My Anger

Living with monsters

Pointing fingers

Where do I begin?

It is not my fault

Being Accountable

No One sees my effort

How do I start?

Starting tomorrow today

The mirror's reflection

Reclaiming You (Your Chapter in the book)

If there is no enemy within, the enemy outside can do you no harm

My Anger

I held onto my anger like a badge of courage for many years. My anger has only been an anchor in my life, weighing me down and keeping me away from all the things I wanted to achieve.

How can you discover or embrace love, joy or happiness when you allow anger to be the dark cloud that rains on your day? I needed to learn how to ask myself this one question.

Why is it so easy for me to hate when the one thing that I would give almost anything to have is love? My anger is the most significant sacrifice that I must be willing to make to obtain the joy and pleasure of love.

I have dreamed of love and me smiling and laughing because of the joy it brought into my life, but when I look in the mirror, I see that image that people told me was not worthy of love, so I retreat to the one thing: I know. **(Pain)**

I stray away from my desire for love, and I embrace my dear friend's anger and hate. They have been my companions for so long that I don't know how I would ever function without them in my life.

Living with Monsters

You can spend a lifetime looking inside the mirror and not truly recognize or understand the image staring back at you. Regrettably, the reflection in the mirror you see is the image that other people may feel about you instead of how you feel about yourself.

Unfortunately, the principle of knowing thyself does not register with a person who never had a chance to get to see the beauty they have within because of the horror the world has shown them.

You can spend a lifetime trying to replace or remove that monster staring down in the depth of your soul, attacking the parts of you that are innocent and pure until the hurt and pain is the only thing that remains.

That monster that started as a reflection has now become the protection of that small part of you that still needs guarding if you hope to save the real you from dying.

That monster lashes out and attacks everything in sight. The mindset of that monster is that I will hurt you before you have the chance of destroying me.

The angriest people tend to have fragile hearts. Let me say this another way. The most enraged people tend to have a delicate soul.

(I know this from experience)

How many times can a heart or soul be broken until it does not heal or mend properly? Even though people with high confidence can say that they are not easily broken, all things are possible given the right circumstances and time.

Time will change everything because change is the only certainty in life.

I was weak before I ever learned how to be strong. I was angry before I had the time to understand what love is. I developed hatred before I learned the power of forgiveness.

I was a broken soul

I lacked in many areas in my life because long before I had a chance to embrace my life, my life displayed everyone else's image of my life but mine.

True strength comes from being tested and surviving those tests. What about those people who were challenged long before they knew that they were fighting for their life?

I feel that strength and courage are given to the mighty to protect the weak until they are strong enough to defend themselves.

What happens when the people in place to safeguard a child only succeed in turning them into a monster? That person will become the reflection of those people who hurt them. The victim of the abuse became destroyed by someone they loved.

Now for them, love has become the pain that they show the world. Anger is the statement from that monster that has now emerged.

Hurt people hurt other people

I find no words more actual than this. My understanding leads me to feel the following way:

Love begets love while pain begets pain. Only love and time can heal the most profound hurt from all the pain.

It takes many small moments of love to heal a lifetime of pain.

Pointing Fingers

Your failure or your success begins and ends with you. When you decide to point the finger at someone else for why your life is not going the way you would like it to go, count how many fingers are pointing back at you when you assign blame to someone else. —three out-numbers one no matter how you look at it.

Only you can give someone else the power to control you and how you react to the challenges that life presents you with on your journey.

Your path to happiness is a long and winding road. If you are willing to stay the course, you will find that your journey was worth the trip.

Only you can overcome your fears and doubts and replace them with the faith and hard work to move the barriers that stand before you.

The decisions you make in life are your cross to bear and no one else.

So, stop shifting blame to others for your life being less than you desire. Hold yourself accountable for all the decisions that you make when it comes to your life. —three out-numbers one no matter how you look at it.

Where do I begin?

Life begins when we start to embrace the gift of life and not focus on the problems or challenges that life brings our way.

To be anxious is to have anxiety about something that has not happened yet in your life. In these moments, you need to trust and pray that everything will be okay.

We must develop a mindset that the trials and tribulations we are going through will not break us. All the obstacles that we face in our lives prepare us to become the best version of ourselves because we have met the worse version of ourselves and did not settle or accept the image that we saw in the mirror.

I have spent long hours in the mirror staring at my reflection, wondering who was staring back at me. I saw an innocent child replaced by a youth's image whose anger and pain haunted him for years.

I saw the image of a teenage boy wondering whether he will live to see the reflection of an adult man staring back at him in the mirror.

I did come to see that adult image of myself. At first, I was not happy with the image that I saw in the mirror.

Years of heartache, anger, and pain left me staring at an image of myself that filled me with disdain.

It would take me many years to embrace the man that I had become and recognize the image in the mirror. I had to stop running from my true self and learn to take the blame for myself and where I was currently in my life.

Holding myself accountable for my actions was one of the most challenging things that I ever did in my life. The toughest thing that I ever did in my life was learning how to forgive myself for not living up to my full potential.

All change begins and ends from within. The longer it takes us to realize that we cannot blame others for our shortcomings and how we respond to the circumstances in our lives, the longer we will regret seeing the mirror image that has become the reflection of our pain and not our happiness.

It is not my fault

These are the words that a defensive person says when confronted about their actions and sometimes a lack thereof.

I was guilty of this myself for a very long time in my life. Someone else is always the blame when things go wrong in our life.

It took what seems to be a lifetime to understand what the following quote meant and how I could apply it to my life.

If there is no enemy within, the enemy outside can do you no harm

If I am at peace with myself, other people's opinions cannot change how I feel about myself. I know and accept my strength and my flaws. I am a work in progress, and each day I am getting better.

I will be accountable for all my actions.

Being Accountable

Why are we so quick to lash out at other people instead of providing that anger and hate to the one person who deserves it all?

There is no situation in life where someone else deserves all the energy you give to hate and despise them.

You can give all the different excuses you would like to so that you can make that statement untrue, but the fact remains, it is true.

You are the only person standing in the way of you achieving your dreams and goals. You are the only nemesis in your life. Everything and everyone else is merely everything and everyone else that does not matter when it comes to the big picture of your life.

Life is about the reaction more than the action itself. How you choose to respond to the challenges that life presents you with is within your control.

Every time you ball your fist up in anger, you are destroying yourself more than you are hurting someone else.

You cannot fight the whole world with your fists. Your fists will never solve any of your problems because violence is not the answer.

Violence begets violence, hate begets pain, while love is the only thing that will give you peace in your heart and your brain.

As a youth and even into my adult years, I hurt many people. I felt broken on the inside. I lashed out at other people because it was easier for me to show anger towards them than to be upset with myself.

Who looks in the mirror these days and gives themselves a reality check when things are not going their way?

Who looks in the mirror to encourage themselves to keep fighting and pushing forward when times are rough?

Who looks in the mirror and smiles at themselves to let them know that someone appreciates all the hard work and sacrifices they make to become a better version of themselves?

I am trying to become that person I write about in my books because achieving success is not complex as other people make it look.

Once you stop giving yourself a pass in life, you will have a better time with your life. I motivate myself each day by looking in the mirror and telling myself the following words to encourage myself:

My life is beautiful today, and it is going to be even better tomorrow because I am making plans today to make it possible

To enjoy the fruits and vegetables of your harvest, you must plant and grow your food before the winter comes.

A farmer never curses the ground; he or she hopes to produce the harvest to survive through the winter months.

A farmer does not fight the land; they work the land to produce the harvest they want to achieve.

Your life is the harvest that your faith and hard work will produce, or your life will show what happens when your actions do not fulfill the promises you made with your words to become a better version of you.

No one sees my effort

We stop trying to improve ourselves and our lives because of how we feel when others don't recognize our effort.

It seems that our faults and shortcomings stand out while the things we do to improve and show growth is ignored by others.

Reality Check

The only person who needs to see and recognize your effort to become a better version of yourself is looking back at you when you stare in the mirror.

Yes, it is nice to have other people give us praise for the things that we do, but the reality is that self-gratitude is the only thing we should come to crave.

Who are you going to give credit to when everything in your life is going well? Who are you going to reward with jewelry and material things when your ship finally comes in?

If that person is you, you must learn to accept the fault that comes with your lack of effort to change your current situation.

That old "Attaboy" you expect for doing all the things you are supposed to do will come in the form of growth and development if you trust the process and keep pushing forward.

People may not recognize the effort it took you to get to the top of the mountain, but they will see you when you are standing on top of the mountain shouting "**Victory**."

Your journey will require you to walk by faith and not by sight because your eyes may wander and take you off your path.

Your path is a journey you will take by yourself. You will have to learn to motivate and encourage yourself along the way.

Each step you take will reveal the effort you used to get closer to your dreams. The progress may be tiny, but over time it will be very effective.

You don't have to be great to get started, but you do have to get started to be great.

Get Moving Forward

How Do I start?

It would help if you learned to command your life. Hard work, long hours, and little sleep is what it will take to be successful. Your body will respond when you decide to act.

You must commit and sacrifice to doing something that can change your life for the better. Commit to changing the mirror's reflection into an image that you recognize and accept as being you.

All successful people understand and accept the following:

The answer to your most challenging problems begins with a straightforward question. Are you ready? Are you prepared to change?

Find what makes your heart sing and create your music. Knowing who you are is the best defense against who you think you are.

Your distress about life might mean you have been living for the wrong reason, not that you have no basis for living.

You cannot dream yourself into a character; you must hammer and forge yourself into one. Commit to change yourself.

When it comes to the question of your life, you are the only answer.

You are the only answer to the problems in your life, and you are the only solution that will make it right. You are the reason for your success or your failure.

> **No question is so difficult to answer as that to which the answer is so apparent.**

How Bad Do You want It?

(No Pressure, it's only your life that's on the line)

If life was a book; The books worth reading are precisely those that challenge your convictions. So now the question becomes a question that only you can answer. Will you take the time to open the book?

Who will you discover when you flip through the pages of your life? Will, you put off reading the book until tomorrow?

> Waiting for tomorrow, it will quickly become today.

Starting tomorrow today

Procrastination is the biggest roadblock to achieving your dreams.

When we procrastinate, we start a chain reaction that only has a negative impact on our life. How can we finish anything that we have yet to start?

When we must face many unfinished tasks, it can be overwhelming both physically and mentally. This undesired strain/ pressure that we put on ourselves can leave us facing many insecurities about ourselves.

Insecurities breeds doubt. Our doubts and insecurities give birth to anger, hate & disappointment, which becomes the reflection we see in the mirror.

Our self-esteem dictates how we feel about ourselves, and, unfortunately for many people, they worry about how other people view them.

As I mentioned before:

If there is no enemy within, the enemy outside can do you no harm

It will take time to change years of self-doubt and insecurities that have build-up over the years. We have to start the process of rebuilding our self-esteem today so that we can be in a better place tomorrow.

What if people don't like the person that I am becoming?

You should be worried about your progress instead of trying to impress people you don't even like. Someone who is against you will be against you. No matter what you do.

The only time they will lose interest in you is when you decide to stop fighting for your life. Only you can make the path that you live, by your effort or lack thereof.

Yes, when you choose not to act, you are still deciding.

As I mentioned before:

If there is no enemy within, the enemy outside can do you no harm

The mirror's reflection

Looks will change, but what is within you will always remain. These are words from a man who was blessed enough to become an older man.

As a youth, the wisdom needed to understand knowledge was not a gift or skill that I fully mastered or comprehended. Youth think that they will have tomorrow to make things right in their lives, but those who understand that our time here on earth is limited cherish every moment.

We spend so much time looking in the mirror, trying to change the reflection that we see, not realizing that the image we see many times is how we think the world sees us.

You will never find true happiness trying to please anyone but yourself. How can anyone who did not make you tell you what you are supposed to look like when you stare in the mirror?

> When people tell me that I am ugly, I smile and say," *But I feel fantastic!*"

Somebody will love you for the person you are if you give them a chance to meet the real you. We waste so much time trying to become what other people will accept that we forget to focus on all the principles we will accept in our life.

It is challenging to teach a child the concept that true beauty comes from within when the world is constantly judging us by our outer appearance.

That child's beauty disappears, trying to live up to the worlds' standards of beauty, not realizing that people with their own insecurities are judging them.

We spend so much money trying to look good, but it leaves us feeling bad because it's expensive to keep up with the Kardashians on a minimum wage budget.

So, now our young ladies try to imitate the lifestyle of the rap group "City-Girls" and still wonder why men disrespect them. Disrespect happens because you stop demanding respect for yourself and choose to become a follower of women who sold you on a lifestyle so they could make money from you.

It's is no different for our young men. They watch rap videos and see artists flashing money and guns but don't realize that most people don't live their portraying lifestyle. The people who try to live the lifestyle they are showing end up in jail or prison if they are lucky. The Feds and the IRS are watching the same videos that you are viewing.

No one is more gangster or ruthless than Uncle Sam. He can commit murder and crimes then pass a law saying that you can't do now what he/they did to get so much power and control.

We spend so much time letting the media and society control us while still claiming to be leaders or different from everyone else.

Our young Kings and Queens need to learn to fix their crowns and tiaras when they stare in the mirror.

Heavy lies the Crown, but it is worth the weight

Most of the media's images are trying to sell you on enhancing the beauty you already have. These qualities and features you are already born possessing. Everything that the media once claimed was ugly and unattractive is what people are now spending thousands of dollars to imitate. No amount of money can change or improve how you feel on the inside.

Reclaiming You (Your Chapter in the book)

This is where you begin writing your journey that will become your testimony of how you claimed victory from within

If there is no enemy within, the enemy outside can do you no harm

If there is no enemy within, the enemy outside can do you no harm

If there is no enemy within, the enemy outside can do you no harm

If there is no enemy within, the enemy outside can do you no harm

If there is no enemy within, the enemy outside can do you no harm

If there is no enemy within, the enemy outside can do you no harm

www.ingramcontent.com/pod-product-compliance
Lightning Source LLC
Chambersburg PA
CBHW071339190426
43193CB00042B/2045